Date: 4/4/14

J 332.024 BUL
Bullard, Lisa.
Brody borrows money /

cloverleaf books™

Money Basics

Brody Borrows Money

Lisa Bullard

illustrated by Mike Byrne

M MILLBROOK PRESS · MINNEAPOLIS

For Mom and Dad —L.B.
For Nat —M.B.

Millbrook Press
A division of Lerner Publishing Group, Inc.
241 First Avenue North
Minneapolis, MN 55401 U.S.A.

Website address: www.lernerbooks.com

Main body text set in Slappy Inline 18/28.
Typeface provided by T26.

Library of Congress Cataloging-in-Publication Data

Bullard, Lisa.
    Brody borrows money / by Lisa Bullard ; illustrated by Mike
Byrne.
        p.   cm. — (Cloverleaf books™ — money basics)
    Includes index.
    ISBN 978-1-4677-0763-3 (lib. bdg. : alk. paper)
    ISBN 978-1-4677-1695-6 (eBook)
    1. Finance, Personal—Juvenile literature. 2. Loans,
Personal—Juvenile literature. I. Byrne, Mike, 1979– illustrator
II. Title.
HG179.B819295 2014
332.7'43—dc23   2012047850

Manufactured in the United States of America
1 – BP – 7/15/13

TABLE OF CONTENTS

Chapter One
Field Trip Find

My friend Josh held out a cool rock. "Look, Brody! My mom said I could buy one thing from the gift shop. I got this."

"I wish I could buy this shiny one," I said. "But it costs **$11.00**. My dad only gave me **$6.00**."

Josh held out some money. "I didn't spend all of mine. **Do you want to borrow some?**"

"Wow, thanks!" I said.

How many dollars more does Brody need?

Dad picked Josh and me up from school. I told him about the field trip and my great new rock. "I'm glad you had fun," he said. "How much did you spend?"

"Only $11.00," I said. "You gave me $6.00, and Josh gave me $5.00."

We pulled up to Josh's house. Dad gave him $5.00. "Here's your money back, Josh. Thanks for giving Brody a loan," he said.

After Josh left, Dad said, "Brody, I gave you $6.00 for the field trip. That was all I wanted you to spend. Now I've had to give Josh $5.00 more. Can you pay me back at home?"

I looked at my rock. It didn't seem so great anymore. I shook my head. "My piggy bank is empty."

Do you save money in something like a piggy bank?

Chapter Two

The Cost of Borrowing

When we got home, Dad showed me a plastic card.

"This is a credit card," he said. "I use it to buy things."

"That's great," I said. "You don't need money."

Dad smiled. "I do need money! When I use the card, I'm borrowing money from the credit card company. But they want me to pay them back. They send me a bill every month."

"What if your piggy bank is empty and you can't pay right away?" I asked.

"Then they charge me interest," Dad said. "That means they add money to what I owe them. Since I don't want to pay extra, I need to pay my bill on time. So I don't buy everything I want."

"How much interest would they charge me for borrowing $5.00?" I asked.

"Different cards charge different amounts," said Dad. "But it might be around 75 cents."

"Uh-oh," I said. "I'll never borrow money again!"

"The important thing is to think hard before you buy something. And then borrow only what you can pay back." Dad stood up. "Follow me."

Brody needs 20 quarters to pay back his $5.00. How many more quarters would he need to pay 75 cents in interest?

Chapter Three

Borrowers All Around

We stepped outside. Dad said, "Most of our neighbors borrowed money to buy these houses. That's the only way many families can afford a house."

"Us too?" I asked.

"Us too," said Dad. "I picked a small house. I knew I could pay the money back that way. I pay some every month. But it's going to take many years. So I'll pay a lot of interest too."

Chapter Four

Pay Back

"Are you going to charge me interest on the $5.00?" I asked.

Have you ever borrowed money?
Did you pay it back?

Dad laughed. "No interest this time. You can pay me back by raking. Then we'll be even."

There sure were a lot of leaves. "I'm going to be as old as my rock by the time I bag all these leaves," I said. "Next time I'll think harder before I borrow money I can't pay back!"

Are there chores you do
to earn money?

Buy with an IOU

Sometimes when a person borrows money from a friend or a family member, he or she writes an IOU note. That stands for "I owe you." The note is a promise to pay the other person back. Sometimes the borrower pays the person back with money. Sometimes the borrower pays the person back by doing some work. Either way, if you borrow money using an IOU, remember: you will have to pay back the loan!

You will want to start by borrowing a small amount of money. Maybe you could ask a parent for enough to buy a package of gum. Then talk with your parent about a job you could do. Maybe you could clear the dinner table next week? Or maybe you could dust the living room this weekend? Together, decide what would be a fair trade for the money you are borrowing.

Once you have decided, make your IOU. Here is an IOU that Brody made after talking with his dad:

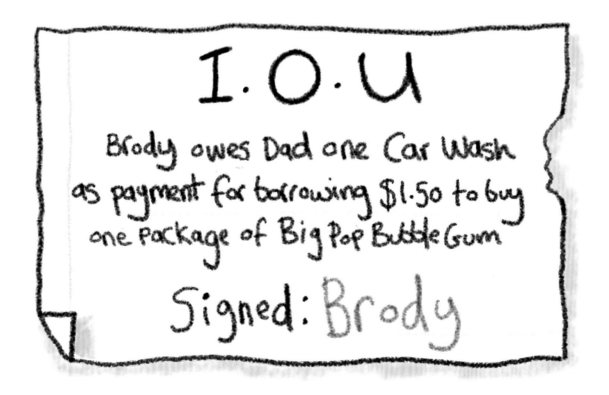

GLOSSARY

afford: to have enough money to pay for an item

bank: a place to save money or do other money business

bill: a written list of what a person has bought and the money he or she owes

borrow: to take money from somebody with the agreement that you will pay it back

charge: to ask for payment

chores: the everyday jobs that members of a family do

credit card: a plastic card that can be used to borrow money to pay for things

interest: an extra charge on borrowed money

loan: money given to a person with the agreement that the money will be paid back

owe: to need to pay someone back

ANSWER KEY

page 5: $5.00

page 15: 3

BOOKS

Cleary, Brian P. *A Dollar, a Penny, How Much and How Many?* Minneapolis: Millbrook Press, 2012.
Rhyming text and goofy illustrations introduce U.S. bills and coins.

Larson, Jennifer S. *Do I Need It? Or Do I Want It? Making Budget Choices.*
Minneapolis: Lerner Publications Company, 2010.
This book teaches you more about making smart spending choices.

Milway, Katie Smith. *One Hen: How One Small Loan Made a Big Difference.*
Tonawanda, NY: Kids Can Press, 2008.
Read this story about an African boy named Kojo who borrowed a little but did a lot with the loan.

WEBSITES

Giving Vicki Credit
http://www.umsl.edu/~wpockets/clubhouse/library/GivingVickiCredit/01.htm
Follow along with Money Mouse in this online story to learn more about good borrowing habits.

Sense and Dollars: The Scoop on Credit
http://senseanddollars.thinkport.org/spending/credit_scoop.html
Check out this website from Maryland Public Television for more lessons about credit. The Charge! game gives visitors a chance to figure out how much different items cost with interest.

LERNER ☑ SOURCE™
Expand learning beyond the printed book. Download free, complementary educational resources for this book from our website, www.lerneresource.com.